D1055407

Martial Arts Masters

Jet Li

Christy Marx

The Rosen Publishing Group, Inc.
New York

To Randy, LOML
And with thanks to Sensei Devito, Sensei Seidel, Sensei
Jordan, and Sifu Arteaga for their teaching and inspiration

Published in 2002 by The Rosen Publishing Group, Inc.
29 East 21st Street, New York, NY 10010

Copyright © 2002 by The Rosen Publishing Group, Inc.

First Edition

Library of Congress Cataloging-in-Publication Data

Marx, Christy.
Jet Li / by Christy Marx.—1st ed.
p. cm. — (Martial arts masters)
Includes bibliographical references and index.
Summary: A biography of the Asian film star and martial
arts master Jet Li, including action photographs and a
listing of his films.
ISBN 0-8239-3519-1
1. Li, Jet—Juvenile literature. 2. Motion picture actors and
actresses—China—Biography—Juvenile literature. 3. Martial
artists—China—Biography—Juvenile literature. [1. Li, Jet. 2.
Actors and actresses. 3. Martial artists.] I. Title. II. Series.
PN2878.L34 M37 2002
91.43'028'092—dc21

2001003610

Manufactured in the United States of America

Table of Contents

In the last decade, Jet Li has emerged as a giant on the international martial arts scene.

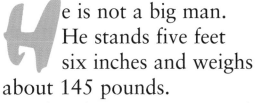

He is not a big man. He stands five feet six inches and weighs about 145 pounds.

When he moves, it is with the fluid grace and power of a wushu master.

His arms move with a blinding speed. His strikes and blocks are used with a blur of precision.

He leaps and soars through the air, whirling, landing with feline agility. His kicks are a deadly dance.

Then he pauses, one hand forward, palm up, the other hand back and poised, his balance perfect, his power held utterly still and ready like a coiled snake.

His dark eyes are intent, never wavering. His face may be cold and lethal. Or he may be smiling, with a taunt to lure his opponent into making the wrong move.

This is the Jet Li of the movies. Movies are make-believe, though, right? Is he really that good? Let's find out.

Chapter 1

A Most Excellent Boy

Jet Li was born Li Lian Jie (sometimes spelled Lee Lian Jie) on April 26, 1963, in Beijing, the capital of the People's Republic of China. He has two older brothers and two older sisters. When he was only two years old, his father died, leaving the family to struggle on its own. His mother had to take a job selling bus tickets to support her children.

Lian Jie felt a keen difference between himself and those schoolmates who had both parents. "That's why I always tried so hard

Jet Li grew up in Beijing, China, under the leadership of Mao Zedong.

when I was young," he said. His father's death also made him very close to his mother.

Early Years

Jet Li described himself as a well-behaved, obedient little boy. In school, the teachers loved him and he always got perfect grades. As the youngest boy in his family, he was pampered and protected by his mother, who wouldn't let him do anything risky, like swimming, ice skating, or even riding a bicycle. Lian Jie didn't get to ride a bicycle until he was nearly fifteen!

He started wushu training in the summer of 1971, when he was eight. Wushu was one of several types of sports offered in summer school to keep kids busy and out of trouble. Lian Jie didn't even know what wushu was, but kids weren't given a choice. They were told to do it, so they did it.

Wushu is not a martial art in itself. Around 1955, the Chinese government formally adopted "wu shu" as the official name applied to a standardized program of Chinese martial arts. Literally translated, *wu* means "military," and *shu* means art. The ancient styles were trimmed to what was considered acceptable to be taught. Here is a simplified summary:

- Bare-handed exercises, which include a long list of styles, such as shaolinquan, zhaquan, huaquan, paoquan, changquan, taijiquan, nanquan, xingyiquan, baguazhang, monkey style, tiger style, eagle style, bear style, and many others.

- Weapon exercises using spears, cudgels, swords, hooks, whips, staffs, darts, and others.

- Partner exercises with two or more persons performing, either bare-handed or using weapons.

- Group exercises by three or more persons, sometimes using music.

Lian Jie was the youngest of only twenty kids out of a thousand who were singled out for special training after that summer. He was enrolled in the Beijing Amateur Sports School. This was a big honor that made him feel special—until he realized it meant staying after school and working another two hours when everybody else got to go home and play.

About the Name "Jet Li"

A language can have different dialects. For example, there is American English, British English, and Australian English. In China, there are many dialects, but two are the most important. Mandarin (called Putonghua) is the official dialect of mainland China. Cantonese is the dialect spoken in Hong Kong and most Chinese movies.

Both dialects are written using the same Chinese characters (called pictographs).

With Chinese names, the last name comes first, so "Li" (李) is Li Lian Jie's last, or family, name. His given name is made up of two Chinese characters, Lian Jie (連杰). But Li Lian Jie's name is pronounced quite differently in the two dialects.

In Putonghua, his name is **Li Lian Jie.**

In Cantonese, his name is **Li Nin Kit** (or Lee Nin Git).

When Lian Jie made his first movie, the producers wanted to arrange his name the English way for the credits, meaning putting the family name last. His name appeared as Lian Jie Li. It was then shortened to Jie Li.

"Then my career took off and they said it was like a jet engine, so they changed Jie Li to Jet Li."

Jet implies great speed and power— a perfect name for someone like Jet Li.

In addition to the honor of being chosen, the government provided a little extra money and clothes for the young athletes, so Lian Jie was able to help out his family.

He worked hard at his wushu and was rewarded by being selected for an even smaller group that advanced further in their training.

The training got harder. In the winter, they had to practice outside some of the time because there wasn't enough indoor space for sports training, and winters in northern China can get very cold. One of the things Lian Jie had to practice were handslaps. He describes it as a no-win situation. If he slapped his hands hard enough to make a sound, his hands hurt like crazy from the cold. But if he didn't slap his hands hard enough to make a sound, he got in trouble with the coach.

Master and Student

Lian Jie's coach, Wu Bin, became a very important figure in the boy's life. At first, Lian Jie didn't understand why Wu Bin was so strict with him.

What his teammates had to do once in training, Lian Jie had to do three times. Wu Bin was not being cruel, though. He saw that the boy had special talent and pushed him harder than the other students.

This method of teaching, where the teacher is harder on the better student, is an ancient tradition. It's a way for the teacher to test how serious and determined a student really is. Wu Bin describes it this way: "A resounding drum must be struck with a heavy hammer."

Yet when Wu Bin realized Lian Jie was lacking strength, he went to the family home and discovered that the family did not think it was healthy to eat meat. He convinced them the growing boy needed protein, and he helped the family by bringing them food.

A class of young children go through the routines of their martial arts training in Beijing, China. Jet Li began training when he was eight years old.

Nowadays, people like to call Jet Li a prodigy, someone who just naturally had a genius for wushu. He finds this very annoying. He worked hard to achieve his skills, and there were times he thought about giving up. He said, "It was my coach, Wu Bin, who helped me steer clear of all obstacles and encouraged me never to give up."

Wushu Training

Lian Jie's training included many styles and techniques, such as the swift and flexible changquan (or longfist), the brisk and light monkey boxing, the vigorous and powerful nanquan, the sweeping arm movements of tongbeiquan, the energetic gun boxing, the serene and circular taijiquan, and the eighteen arms.

Within wushu there are two major divisions of styles, called internal and external, or sometimes soft and hard, or static and dynamic.

The hard/dynamic/external style refers to martial arts such as Shaolin kung fu, karate, and styles in which more direct force is used, and depends more on physical strength. For example, an incoming punch would be met by a strong block.

In the soft/static/internal styles, the punch would be deflected away with as little effort as is needed. Internal martial arts draw power from within, through control of breathing and channeling of life energy. When done right, they are very powerful indeed. Taijiquan and aikido are examples of internal styles.

Taijiquan (also spelled t'ai chi ch'uan) is done using extreme slow

Taijiquan

Taijiquan involves more than just learning the physical moves. It's a complex system using balance, continuous shifting of weight, breathing skills, controlling internal energy, and building muscle memory.

It is said that a taijiquan expert can overcome a weight of 1,000 pounds by applying a force of four ounces.

motion. Jet Li uses taijiquan techniques within his wushu. "You see me concentrating and thinking about the next move and the movement is graceful, almost like dancing."

The eighteen arms technique required training with weapons. The weapons students learned to use were the sabre, spear, sword, halberd, ax, battle-ax, hook, fork, whip, mace,

A martial arts instructor leads a young student through traditional exercises. The best students undergo the most rigorous, often grueling, training.

hammer, talon, trident-halberd, cudgel, long-handled spear, short cudgel, stick, and meteor hammer.

Young Champion

When he was nine years old, Lian Jie prepared for his first competition. There were no first, second, or third places or prizes. There was just one award for excellence given to the best performer. The competitors came from all over China. Lian Jie won.

At his next big performance, he got to meet the premier, the head of his country. It was a very big deal, like getting to

Elderly men practice wushu near the Forbidden City in Beijing.

personally meet the president. This is how important the Beijing Wushu Team was becoming in China.

No Time to Be a Kid

Lian Jie's training became even more intense. In fact, he was cut back to having to attend school for only half a day, and finally not at all. Lian Jie trained in wushu full-time. He lived in a dormitory at the sports school and trained all week. He was able to go home on Saturday, but he had to be back by Sunday night.

Jet Li's word for the training is "bitter." A typical day went like this: The students were woken by a bell at 6:00 AM. They had only ninety seconds to get dressed and be ready at attention. They had an hour of practice and a break to eat breakfast and brush their teeth, and then they went back to practice at 8:30 until noon. They had a short rest after lunch, unless they were suddenly called upon to perform for visiting tourists, which happened a lot. After dinner, at 7:30 PM, they went back to training for another three hours, and then to bed. They had a total of eight hours of training a day. Tough work!

Once, their coach made them work out at night, in the dark. This was terrible because no one could ever be sure where the coach with his flashlight was. Instead of being able to relax a little when the coach was looking somewhere else, they had to keep working perfectly or they might get caught slacking off.

Lian Jie was working so hard he somehow stepped wrong and felt a terrible pain in his foot, but he didn't

dare stop or complain about it.
Nobody liked to complain. If you
said an arm hurt, the coach made you
do a thousand kicks instead.

He kept training on his badly
swollen foot for another two days
before a teacher finally noticed.
Then they found out he had a
cracked bone in his foot! They put
him in a plaster cast that nearly
covered his entire leg. Even this
didn't halt his practice.

Every day, he was carried out on
a teammate's back and had to
practice hand and arm moves
instead. Broken foot or not, he
had to practice for eight hours.

For three years, Lian Jie's life
was all about wushu. Finally, at age
eleven, he would embark on a series
of adventures around the world that
would change his life.

Chapter 2

Seeing a Whole New World

In 1974, Lian Jie was chosen as one of the thirty best wushu athletes in the country. This special group was forged into a team that would travel to other countries on goodwill tours and demonstrate the art of wushu. But the group was intended to be more than just an athletic team. For decades, China had sealed itself off from outside influences and foreign visitors. Now it was slowly opening up and thawing its cold relationship with the rest of the world. The wushu team was to help this thaw by representing their country abroad.

The Wide World

For a whole year, the Beijing Wushu Team was put through an additional kind of training just as tough as wushu—how to behave in a Western country. They had to learn how to use knives and forks, how to answer a telephone, how to behave in a crowd—all sorts of details about how to act in countries totally different from their own.

The team gave demonstrations in four American cities: Honolulu, San Francisco, New York, and Washington, D.C. The whole time that they were in the United States, they were protected by American bodyguards—

one guard for every two of the forty-four Chinese boys and girls.

By now, Lian Jie was no longer a quiet, meek little boy. He had become very playful. He liked to tease his bodyguard. He suspected the bodyguards really knew how to speak Chinese even though they pretended they couldn't. So he said to his bodyguard urgently in Chinese, "I have to go to the bathroom!" The bodyguard, without thinking, answered him in Chinese and was very embarrassed to get caught this way. Lian Jie had a good laugh at how well his trick had worked.

One of the first things these well-trained kids saw, to their shock, was how informal Americans were about manners and eating. None of the rules the kids had been taught were being used. Sometimes the guards would even grab chicken with their hands! Lian Jie was starting to see that what he had been taught didn't always match up to the way things were.

He had been taught that only Chinese things were good and everything about America was bad. But at eleven years old, he quickly saw that Americans were nice people who cared about the safety of him and his friends, and that life in America was really pretty good. Jet Li said, "It was difficult for me to believe in my heart what the adults had been teaching us: that all Americans were class enemies who couldn't be trusted."

One day when Lian Jie was feeling silly, he wondered if his hotel room had actually been bugged, so he went around to parts of the room and talked to objects like the mirror and flower vase. He said he wanted chocolate, bananas, and ice cream. When he got back that night, he found chocolate, bananas, and ice cream in his room. He asked around and found out he was the only one who got the treats. He was a lot more careful with what he said after that!

Lian Jie received a little money during his tour, about five dollars a day. But he didn't waste it or spend it on himself. Instead, he saved it up and bought his mother a luxury that was almost unknown in China then, especially for an average person. He bought her a genuine Swiss watch. She was thrilled.

Star Power

The highlight of the tour came at the end when the team gave a wushu demonstration on the lawn of the White House for President Richard

President Richard Nixon laughs as he talks with Chinese children wearing Mao Zedong buttons in Hangchow, China, during his visit in 1972.

Nixon and other officials. Afterward, Nixon said to Lian Jie, "Young man, your kung fu is very impressive. How about being my bodyguard when you grow up?"

Without thinking about it, Lian Jie blurted out, "No, I don't want to protect any individual. When I grow up, I want to defend my one billion Chinese countrymen!"

That patriotic statement made him a hero and celebrity when he got back to China. After that, he found himself involved in any event where special guests had to be greeted, and he met Presidents Gerald Ford and Jimmy Carter when they visited China in later years.

What Is Kung Fu?

Nowadays, one associates the term "kung fu" with Chinese martial arts consisting of punches, kicks, and a certain style of fighting. The original meaning of kung fu, however, had to do with the time and energy spent in learning something. The literal translation is "skill from effort." Anything you work hard at over a period of time in order to develop skill can be called your kung fu.

There is one theory that the term "kung fu" first became widely known in the mid-1800s, when huge numbers of Chinese men came to the United States during and after the gold rush.

But the popular use of the term as we know it today came from Bruce Lee. He used the term when talking about his own efforts to become skilled in martial arts. His use of the word was misunderstood. People came to think it meant the style of martial arts he was doing. The term has stuck. Now it is so strongly associated with certain martial arts (mainly those from the Shaolin Temple) that it would be hard to change it.

A more correct spelling of the phrase is "gung fu." The pronunciation is more like a hard "g" in the word "good" rather than a "k." For this reason, you may also come across references to "gung fu" as well as "kung fu." They both mean the same thing: skill from effort.

Back Home

One of the most important lessons Lian Jie learned as this first tour came to an end was that people from very different cultures can form strong and lasting friendships. The American bodyguards had become very fond of the Chinese children. Toward the end of the visit, the bodyguards disobeyed orders not to speak in Chinese and told the kids in their own language how much they had come to like them. Everyone— boys and girls, kids and adults—cried when it was time to say good-bye.

Back home again, Lian Jie entered serious training for the huge National Games. They were like the Olympics but held within China for Chinese athletes only. He was only twelve years old, but because of his ability and the fact that he'd won a major competition, he was allowed to compete against the adults.

Wu Bin began to bring other respected teachers and trainers to work with Lian Jie, including ancient masters like the ninety-seven-year-old Wu Tu Nan. Lian Jie learned from whomever he could, even from Beijing opera actors and dancers. He was always looking for ways to improve his style and performance. He invented a training device he called "beating stars." It was simple and clever. Lian Jie suspended soccer balls on tight ropes between trees so that he was surrounded by them on four sides. Then he would strike each ball to make it bounce, moving from ball to ball, keeping in continuous motion. "It practices the hands, eyes, body, and feet to be swift and fast, turning and responding," he said.

During a qualifying round for the National Games, Lian Jie had an accident that had a spectacular effect on everyone watching. He was demonstrating a routine with a broadsword and, without realizing it, sliced his head open at the beginning of the

Chinese gymnasts stand in formation after performing for President Richard Nixon during his visit to Beijing, China, in 1972.

routine. But he was so well trained and so focused inside that he just thought he was sweating a lot! As he said, "I kept going—punching, rolling, leaping. I didn't feel any pain."

After he finished, he saw that he was drenched in blood and was rushed to the hospital to get stitches. His mother was terribly upset.

Three days later, even with a head full of stitches, Lian Jie returned for the final qualifying round and won. He beat out two other competitors in their twenties! Between 1974 and 1979, he won the title of Men's All-Around National Wushu Champion five times.

Goodwill Tours

In 1976, the wushu team went on more goodwill tours to cities all over

Europe, Asia, Africa, and the Middle East. One of the hard things to cope with was the terrible heat in Iraq and Africa, up to 122 degrees Fahrenheit (50 degrees Celsius). The athletes would pour water on their beds to make them cool enough to sleep on and perform at night when it was slightly cooler.

One night, Lian Jie grabbed what he thought was a soda from a cooler full of ice. He guzzled it all down and then felt so dizzy and goofy he couldn't perform. It turned out he had just drunk half a bottle of champagne.

The team did not always travel in style. On one journey in Africa, they had to share a cargo plane with herds of sheep and cattle. They often had to ride in old planes that threatened to crash.

Jet Li's Wushu Awards

1974: Chinese National Youth Sports Competition Winner

    All around champion

    Optional fist form champion

    Broadsword champion

1974: Chinese Men's All-Around National Wushu Champion

    Fixed fist form champion

    Spear, second place

1975: Chinese Men's All-Around National Wushu Champion

    Fist form champion

    Broadsword champion

1977–1978: Chinese Men's All-Around National Wushu Champion

> All around champion
> Fist form champion
> Broadsword champion
> Fixed fist form champion

1979: Chinese Men's All-Around National Wushu Champion

> All around champion
> Superior fixed fist form champion
> Optional fist form champion
> Broadsword champion
> Sparring form champion

As Li put it, it was quite an education doing those tours.

During that same tour, the team visited the Philippines. They were taken as guests to various stores. One store gave each team member some wonderful clothing and another store gave each of them custom-made leather boots. These were much nicer things than they were used to having, and they were excited about getting them. But the Chinese government had a rule: Athletes could only keep gifts that were under a certain value. The clothes and boots were higher than that value.

The kids were told they couldn't keep the gifts. They would have to turn them in. They were crushed. Being kids, they got mad and decided they would rather destroy their new stuff than turn it over. So they spent a whole day rolling in the dirt, playing rough games of soccer, and ripping and grinding up the clothes and boots.

The next day their coach told them that because they had worked so hard on the tour, the government had made an exception and would let them keep their gifts. The kids couldn't believe it. They glumly left the room and spent the rest of the day trying to restore the tattered gifts. As Li asked when telling this story, "You couldn't have told us earlier? Just one day earlier?"

Chapter 3

Making Movies in China

When he was eleven and already famous, Lian Jie was asked to be in movies, but he was too young. "I ate a lot every day, but it could not help me grow up faster! So until I was seventeen, I waited."

The first movie Lian Jie made when he turned seventeen was called *The Shaolin Temple*. At this point he changed his name to Jet Li for the American audiences. Most Chinese movies were and are still made in Hong Kong. This major city sits on an island off the southern tip of China. While Lian Jie was growing up, Hong Kong was under British rule. It was almost a little country of its own. It only officially became a part of China again in 1997.

Chinese Moviemaking

Hong Kong is to China what Hollywood is to America—the center of moviemaking. *The Shaolin Temple* was unusual because it was made in mainland China instead of Hong Kong.

This meant that the filmmakers didn't know much about how to make a movie. The director would tell the young wushu athletes what the basic story was, then let them go off and work out all the fight scenes on their own. It took a very long

Buddhist monks practice wushu near the Shaolin Monastery in Henan Province, China.

time to make the movie—nearly two years. Because it was a historical movie about the Shaolin monks, the actors had to shave their heads. This was fine for summer, but during the winter, they had very cold heads.

Worse, there was a week of shooting in which Lian Jie had to jump in and out of a river filled with ice floes. He described it like this: "Never before—and never since—have I experienced such intense coldness. You jump into the water, and by the time you surface, you're frozen." It was agony, and after doing this for four days, Lian Jie could no longer open his hands properly. It took a week of medical treatment to regain the use of his hands.

In spite of these hardships, the wushu actors found making a movie much easier than eight hours of tough training.

His next movie was called *Shaolin Kids,* and it was based directly on the stories and experiences of the wushu actors. It was about their lives growing up under this kind of training. But during this movie, they suffered from terrible heat. Sometimes, at the height of noon, they would crack an egg on the ground and time how long it took to cook. The egg was done in just a few minutes.

It was so hot that if someone had to take a fall and put a hand to the ground, it would burn a layer of skin off his hand. The actors had to wet the ground down with water

What Is Shaolin?

Shaolin means "little forest." The first temple was founded in the pine forest of Shaoshi Mountain around AD 500. The monks who studied there became known as Shaolin monks. These monks studied Buddhism, a spiritual philosophy of achieving harmony with the universe and oneself.

Boys would enter between the ages of five and seven, and they did not graduate until they were at least twenty-two. They studied many things besides religion, such as law or medicine.

These studies included numerous forms of martial arts. Shaolin martial arts styles were often based upon observation of how animals moved and defended themselves. The movements of each animal would be adapted to a style named after it, such as tiger, bear, snake, and praying mantis. Other styles were named after a family or a specific person who was famous for developing the forms, such as Wing Chun and Hung Gar.

constantly. During fight scenes, they would get overheated and suddenly topple over from shock.

In some areas where they went to shoot, there wouldn't even be running water. "We lived like the poorest of peasants," Li said.

While making *Shaolin Temple 3*, Lian Jie became aware of the inequality between how the actors and crew members from the mainland were treated, and how the people brought in from Hong Kong were treated. First, the Hong Kong people were paid 150,000 yuen (Chinese money) a day instead of only one or two yuen a day like Lian Jie. They got to buy things mainlanders couldn't buy, like American sodas, and they got special, catered food while the mainlanders had to eat cheap food out of Styrofoam containers. It made Lian Jie so angry he almost quit making movies.

Li the Director

Before Lian Jie could decide to quit moviemaking, he got a chance to direct his very own film. He made a movie called *Born to Defend,* and he used it to express his anger over unequal treatment. He disguised it by telling a story about a historical incident at the end of World War II in which Chinese soldiers were mistreated. The movie didn't do very well, and even Li admitted he didn't achieve what he set out to do. After that, he decided to give up directing and concentrate on being an actor and producer.

Movie Machine

From 1982 to 1998, Li made a total of twenty-seven movies, most of them in Hong Kong. Hong Kong kung fu movies are great fun to see. They are filled with amazing stunts and fantastic fight sequences that sometimes go on for five or ten minutes without a pause, using all sorts of unexpected gimmicks and props. Characters run up walls, fly across rooftops, whirl through the air, and make superhuman jumps— all done with the magic of wirework.

Wirework is a technique perfected by Hong Kong filmmakers (and that has since spread into Hollywood movies such as *The Matrix*). The actor wears a harness under his or her clothes. The wire attaches to the harness, then the actor is lifted on the wire by a crane or other device. The end result is an actor who seems to defy gravity. The wire is then digitally removed from the film during the editing process.

In the late 1980s, Jet Li married an actress named Huang Qiuyan. They had two daughters, but they divorced a couple of years later during a time when Jet Li's career was not doing well.

Then, in 1990, Jet Li made a movie that turned him into an international sensation. It was called *Once Upon a Time in China.* The movie was about a famous historical Chinese hero, Wong Fei-Hung. Li made a couple of sequels to that movie, then opened his own production company and made many great wushu action movies of his own. Some were set in China's recent past, some in the ancient past, and a few in modern times. One was a remake of the American film *The Bodyguard,* with Jet Li playing the Kevin Costner part.

As Hong Kong movies boomed, so did gangster involvement in the moviemaking business. Jet Li's personal manager was gunned down in 1992, and actors were threatened, sometimes at gunpoint,

The poster for *Once Upon a Time in China,* the film
that made Jet Li into an international superstar

to take less money or else. Though he kept making movies, Li began to look toward Hollywood, seeking a way to break in.

His big break finally came in 1998.

Chapter 4

Making Movies in Hollywood

Jet Li's leap into Hollywood movies came when he was cast in the part of a martial arts villain, Wah Sing Ku, in *Lethal Weapon 4*. His audition was very informal: He did a short scene with Mel Gibson and then they chatted for a while.

Li was a big fan of the *Lethal Weapon* movies, so it was difficult for him to think about hitting Mel Gibson. Gibson finally had to tell him, "You can beat me up, no problem."

Li found Gibson to be a perfectionist who was determined to get things just right, even if it meant he had to let Li slam him down on a table for twenty takes. Everyone on the *Lethal Weapon 4* production was warm and friendly to Li. They invited him to contribute his ideas, and they let him import his own stunt people to do the wushu fight scenes the right way.

The Prankster

Before he began the movie, Jet Li had been warned that Gibson was a big practical joker. So one day, Li walked up and surprised Gibson with a trick ring that delivered a buzzing shock. Gibson jumped and said, "Hey! Wait a minute! I never did anything to you!"

Jet Li poses with the main cast members of *Lethal Weapon 4*. From left to right, they are Rene Russo, Danny Glover, Mel Gibson, Joe Pesci, Li, director Richard Donner, and producer Joel Silver.

Later, Gibson got even. He waited until Li was talking to the press using a translator. Li was wearing headphones and his translator was in a booth. Gibson got into the booth, took over the microphone, and began yelling in Li's ear, "He's a liar! He's a liar!" and all sorts of things. Li had to stop the interview and explain there was someone yelling in his ear.

The Hollywood Way

Lethal Weapon 4 was the first time in his long career that Li had ever played a villain. He has been asked many times why he decided to accept that role, and his answer is simply, "Because I am an actor. I think as an actor you should try everything."

He discovered many differences between the way Hollywood and Hong Kong movies were made. In Hong Kong, only a few people made decisions and things would happen quickly. Filmmakers had small budgets, so they couldn't afford fancy sets or models, wouldn't have

Jet Li *(right)* played a rogue in *Lethal Weapon 4*. In this scene, Wah Sing Ku (Li) jostles with Detective Sergeant Martin Riggs (Mel Gibson).

very many cameras, and had to work on a rush schedule sixteen hours a day, seven days a week. There was more action than dialogue, so they usually worked out the story and action, and hired the cast before ever writing a script.

In Hollywood, everything begins with the script. Before anything else can happen, there must be a good script. There are much bigger budgets, many more people involved in all aspects of decision making, up to six or seven cameras used at a time, better sets and effects, and higher safety standards. And wonder of wonders, nobody had to work weekends! For someone as hard-working as Jet Li, this was luxury.

Yet the hardest part of Jet Li's Hollywood experience was learning English. He had no exposure to

English when he was growing up. American movies and music weren't allowed in China when he was a boy. He found it very hard to learn English at the age of thirty-five.

He tackled it with the same energy he shows in his wushu, working with a language teacher. "Life, to me, is a learning process," Li said. "Young or old, you have to keep learning." But he also talked about the frustration of using sentences hundreds of times and still not getting them right, and getting mad with himself when he used a word the wrong way.

The first American-made movie in which he starred is *Romeo Must Die,* a movie with a blend of hip-hop and martial arts action. In this movie, he once again plays the hero. The producer of the movie (who also produced *The Matrix*) said, "With

In *Romeo Must Die*, Li (right) plays an ex-cop who, while investigating the murder of his brother, falls in love with the daughter of a mafia boss and ends up in a turf war between rival mobs.

The Matrix . . . we had to create martial arts sequences aided by special effects. But Jet . . . Jet *is* a special effect."

For Li, the hardest part of making *Romeo* was a scene where he had to hang upside down by a chain around one leg, fighting off prison guards. It took twelve hours a day for five days to finish the scene. After fifty minutes of hanging upside down, he would get a headache and his face would turn red. He'd yell for shooting to stop so he could take a break before doing it all over again. He said later that it was the toughest thing he has done in movies so far.

Image and Family

Li admits it's hard to change his image. People go to his movies

It took five days of filming at twelve hours a day to complete this scene in *Romeo Must Die,* in which Han Sing (Jet Li) fought several prison guards while hanging upside down from a chain around one leg.

because they want to see him do martial arts. He is realistic enough to give the audience what they want. Even so, one day he would like to act in a movie without action and be appreciated as an actor.

He has come a long way from his humble beginnings in China. He earned $3 million for *Romeo* and almost $10 million for *A Tibetan Monk in New York*. But he doesn't count happiness by how much money he makes.

His happiness comes from what he accomplishes and from his new family. Li married former Hong Kong actress Nina Li Chi on September 19, 1999. Notice all the 9s in the date. In China, the number 9 is associated with longevity. Clearly, they want this marriage to last a long time.

Liu Jian (Jet Li) tussles with a couple of villains before rescuing a young girl from an orphanage in *Kiss of the Dragon*.

When asked where he considers home to be, he said, "I love family and believe where my wife likes to stay, that is my home." Li made his wife a promise to stay home and take care of her when she became pregnant. She was pregnant when Li was offered the starring role in *Crouching Tiger, Hidden Dragon*. He turned down the role and the movie went on to become a gigantic hit. He doesn't regret his choice. The lesson, said Li: "A man's word—when you give it, you need to do it." In April 2000, Jet and Nina had a baby girl, Jane Li.

For now, they have settled into a house near Pasadena, California. Li enjoys the freedom of moviemaking that the United States makes possible for him. Despite his American house, he considers himself more of a world citizen than belonging to any one

Jet Li with *Romeo Must Die* costar Aaliyah at the film's premiere in Los Angeles, California, on March 20, 2000. Tragically, Aaliyah died in August 2001.

Jet Li and his wife, actress Nina Li Chi, at the premiere of *Kiss of the Dragon* in Hong Kong on July 6, 2001

country. This goes back to his days as a boy with the Beijing Wushu Team. He traveled to so many countries and experienced so many different ways of life that his attitude became one of appreciation. He appreciates all aspects of a country or a city, both the good sides and the bad sides. He can (and does) find something good to say about any place he visits.

Jet Li is perfectly content to spend months in Paris shooting a movie, then six months shooting a movie in China, and then the rest of his time in America. There's no telling where his career might take him next.

Chapter 5

Jet Li's Advice About Wushu

Jet Li has a very clear idea of how he feels martial arts should be used in the twenty-first century. He believes they are best used:

- To become an Olympic champion

- To become an actor or stuntperson

- To become healthier

- For self-defense

Olympic Sports

One of the main purposes of wushu today is sport competition. For Olympic competitions, Li recommends starting as early as possible, preferably before age thirteen.

Wushu takes a lot of time and devotion. The Beijing Wushu Team trained five to eight hours a day. "Years of inflexible training builds will. If you are always allowed to stop training whenever you feel discomfort, you will find it too easy to give yourself permission to quit," he said.

Li warns students not to concentrate on speed. "Wushu is not a race. It shouldn't be like other sports, where the fastest athlete wins." Instead, concentrate on the internal and on bringing your whole energy together with your mind.

Devotion to wushu requires the understanding of how and why you perform moves.

It is not just about physical action; with wushu, you must also think about everything you do, why you do it, how you do it, and always with the goal to improve yourself.

For Television and Movies

For stunt training, Li thinks you could start later, as late as age eighteen, and still do well after about three years of concentrated training. The trick is to find a good teacher, which usually means someone located in the Los Angeles area.

Stunt work for Hollywood is specialized. One type of stuntperson may do high falls, while another does car driving. Li will do his own stunts if it's his area of skill, such as wushu. But when it's something he doesn't know how to do, like falling off a

Kiss of the Dragon, Jet Li plays a Chinese intelligence
ficer in Paris who, after being framed for murder, must
oid the law while he hunts the real bad guys.

building, he leaves it to a stuntman. "Every actor in the world needs a stuntman to help. I'm a normal guy. I only play the hero."

Li warns that doing wushu for movies can be dangerous. Over the years, he has broken an arm and a leg, and hurt his back. Altogether, he broke seven bones and had many other injuries while making movies. He warns that if you want to make action movies, you have to live with the risk of broken bones.

For Health

Jet Li strongly urges anyone of any age, from seven to seventy, to use wushu or other martial arts to become healthier.

For this purpose, it isn't necessary to train as hard or for

Jet Li in the action-packed *The Black Mask*. Li does most of the martial arts stunts in his movies.

such long periods. Two hours a day can be plenty, or far less than that for someone who is older or has health problems. Taijiquan is especially good for people who may not be quite up to hard training for whatever reason. It is a low-impact style that has excellent results for anyone.

For Self-Defense

Li goes out of his way to point out that wushu should never be used to create fights. He has never used his wushu against another person in real life.

"We never want people learning martial arts to kick somebody somewhere. If somebody uses martial arts fighting on the streets, that's low."

He does his best to avoid conflict, and he advises people to go to the police or a reliable authority if there is trouble. Wushu or any martial art should never be used for violence.

He has never used his wushu for self-defense. If someone came up to rob him, he would ask what the robber wanted and give it to him: his money, his watch, whatever. He points out there is a big difference between what an actor can do in a movie and what someone might be able to do in real life. "A gun outdoes years of martial arts training in a split second."

If you are forced to protect yourself and are facing a larger enemy, Li gives this advice: "Size isn't most important. Your mind and your heart—that's where the

Jet Li poses for a *New York Magazine* photo shoot on June 28, 2001.

power comes from. You can see it in the eyes."

You can certainly see it in the eyes of Jet Li.

Filmography

Movies are sometimes released with more than one title. In this list, "aka"(also known as) denotes a film's alternative title(s).

The Shaolin Temple (1982)

Shaolin Temple 2: Kids from Shaolin (1984)
aka: *Kids from Shaolin, Kids of Shaolin, Shaolin Boys, Shaolin Kids*

Born to Defend (1986)
aka: *Born to Defence*

Martial Arts of Shaolin (1986)
aka: *Shaolin Temple 3: Martial Arts of Shaolin, Arahan, North and South Shaolin*

Dragon Fight (1988)
aka: *Dragon Kickboxer*

Dragons of the Orient (1988)

Abbot Hai Teng of Shaolin (1988)

Once Upon a Time in China (1990)

Once Upon a Time in China 2 (1991)

Swordsman II (1992)

The Master (1992)
aka: *Wong Fei-hung*

Once Upon a Time in China 3 (1992)

Fong Sai Yuk (1993)
aka: *The Legend of Fong Sai Yuk,
The Legend*

Fong Sai Yuk II (1993)
aka: *The Legend II, The Legend of
Fong Sai Yuk 2*

The Last Hero in China (1993)
aka: *Claws of Steel, Deadly China
Hero, Iron Rooster vs. the Centipede*

The Kung Fu Cult Master (1993)
aka: *Kung Fu Master,
The Evil Cult*

The Tai Chi Master (1993)
aka: *Tai-Chi, Twin Warriors*

*Li Lian Jie's Shaolin
Kung Fu* (1994)
(documentary)
aka: *Shaolin Kung Fu*

The New Legend of Shaolin (1994)
aka: *Legend of the Future Shaolin,
Legends of Shaolin, Hung Hei-Koon,
Shaolin's Five Founders*

The Bodyguard from Beijing (1994)
aka: *The Defender*

Fist of Legend (1994)

My Father Is a Hero (1995)
aka: *Jet Li's The Enforcer, Letter to
Daddy*

High Risk (1995)

Black Mask (1996)

Dr. Wei in the Scripture with No Words
(1996)
aka: *Dr. Wai and the Scripture
Without Words, Adventure King,
The Scripture with No Words*

Once Upon a Time in China and America (1997)
aka: OUATICA, *Once Upon a Time in China 6*

Lethal Weapon 4 (1998)

Hitman (1998)
aka: *King of Assassins*

Romeo Must Die (2000)

The One (2001)

Kiss of the Dragon (2001)

Glossary

aikido A style of unarmed self-defense from Japan, with circular motions that redirect an attacker's force. It uses many throwing techniques.

baguazhang A Chinese martial art containing nimble footwork and flexible body swerves.

Buddhism Religion from India, based on the teachings of Buddha, which seeks to end suffering and find enlightenment.

Cantonese A dialect of Chinese spoken in Hong Kong and the Canton province in southern China.

changquan ("northern long fist") A Chinese fighting style with long arm swinging motions, high-standing postures, long whirling kicks, jumps, rolling, tumbling, and swift, nimble movements.

cudgel A long pole used as a weapon.

dialect A regional variation in how a language is spoken.

eighteen arms Eighteen different weapons used in wushu training.

gun boxing A Shaolin Temple boxing style that is fast, rhythmic, and strong.

gung fu Same as kung fu.

halberd A weapon with an axlike blade and a spike at the end of a long pole.

huaquan Chinese martial art that involves a lot of fighting from a position on the ground, with tumbling, sideways attacks, and fast, strong blows.

Hung Gar Derived from a southern Shaolin style, a combination of tiger style and crane style kung fu.

kung fu Literally "skill from effort."

mace Usually a metal ball (sometimes covered with spikes) that is swung by a long chain attached to a strong wooden handle.

Mandarin Dialect of Chinese spoken on mainland China, now the official dialect of the People's Republic of China. Also known as Putonghua.

meteor hammer   A length of rope (fourteen feet long) with an iron or metal ball at the end, used rather like a whip.

monkey boxing   A fighting style based upon the loose, wild, and unpredictable movements of monkeys.

nanquan   An overall name for many types of boxing styles from southern China, generally based on the movements of the tiger, leopard, crane, snake, and dragon.

paoquan   Chinese boxing style known as cannon fist or fire fist.

pictographs   Chinese writing symbols that represent whole words or concepts instead of a specific sound like a letter.

Putonghua   Also known as Mandarin, this is the official dialect of the People's Republic of China.

shaolinquan   A boxing style that uses aggressive movements, with combinations of strikes, kicks, throws, and holds. A shaolinquan boxer is supposed to be as fierce as an attacking tiger.

Shaolin Temple   Place of worship and education in ancient China, inhabited by Shaolin monks.

taijiquan   Chinese martial art in the "internal" style. It teaches overcoming attacks with quiet, gentle moves, taking advantage of the attacker's weaknesses.

taoism   pronounced "dowism," Chinese religion that looks to the order and harmony of nature as the proper way to live.

tongbeiquan ("white ape fist") A Chinese boxing style of sweeping arm movements and whiplike, snapping arm attacks.

trident Long-handled weapon ending in a forklike tip with three sharp prongs.

Wing Chun A martial art founded by a woman in southern China. Correct position, sensitivity, timing, and strategy are emphasized over power.

wushu Literally "martial art," the Chinese government's official name for approved Chinese martial arts.

xingyiquan A Shaolin style that teaches fast attacks at close range using the head, shoulders, elbows, hands, knees, hips, and feet.

zhaquan ("fist of zha") A Moslem-Chinese martial arts style from western China. It is a long-range boxing form that combines hard and soft techniques and many kicks.

For More Information

Web Sites

The Official Jet Li Web site
http://www.jetli.com/index.php
This is a great Web site, the first
place to go to learn about Jet Li,
from Jet Li himself.

More Sites About Jet Li

About.com
http://actionadventure.about.com/
movies/actionadventure/cs/jetli

JetLi Fanworks.com
http://www.jetlifanworks.com/
 index2.html

Netasia.net
http://www.netasia.net/users/sgc_wdi/
 bio.htm

About Jet Li's Movies

Island Video: Jet Li
http://www.islandvideo.net (and
 perform a search for "Jet Li."

MartialArtsMart.com
http://store.yahoo.com/
 martialartsmart

Martial Arts of China magazine
http://www.bambootemple.com/
 shaolinbrand/sx060001.htm

Netasia.com
http://www.netasia.net/users/sgc_wdi/
    whereto.htm

Netflix.com
http://www.netflix.com (and perform
    a search for "Jet Li")

About Chinese Martial Arts

Earthworks Emporium: Tai Mantis
    Kung Fu Association
http://www.earthworks.com/
    eng/index.html

Martialinfo.com
http://www.martialinfo.com/
    MartialMainFrame.htm

Richard Tsims Lau Kune Do
http://www.jps.net/bizmal/
    martial_arts/master_tsim.html

About Taijiquan

Eight Step Praying Mantis Kung Fu
   http://www.8step.com/taiji/
   index.html

About Kung Fu and Shaolin

Martialinfo.com
http://www.martialinfo.com/Martial
   MainFrame.htm

PrayingMantis
http://www.8step.com/mantis/
   index.html

Seven Star Praying Mantis Directory
http://www.authentickungfu.com/
   mantis_directory.html

Shaolin Gung Fu Institute
http://www.shaolin.com/
   styles_shaolin.html

About the Beijing Wushu Team

Limited Infinity Research Center:
  Wushu Styles
http://infinite.org/library/pages/
  SBMAC1.5-233.html
Excellent information about various
styles used in wushu.

Raffi's Wu Shu Page
http://www.beijingwushuteam.com

For Further Reading

There is a book written about Jet Li, *The HKS Guide to Jet Li,* by Chris Ducker and Stuart Cutler. You can order it at this Web site: http://www.hksmag.co.uk/ jetliguide.htm

Cheong Cheng Leong. *Phoenix-Eye Fist: A Shaolin Fighting Art of South China*. New York: Weatherhill, 1997.

Corcoran, John, and Emil Farkes. *The Original Martial Arts Encyclopedia*. Los Angeles: Pro Action Pub., 1993.

Ho'o, Marshall. *Tai Chi Chuan*. Burbank, CA: Ohara Publications, 1989.

Little, John R., and Curtis F. Wong. *Ultimate Martial Arts Encyclopedia*. Lincolnwood, IL: NTC Contemporary Books, 2000.

Prakarsa, Leo Budiman. *Shantung Black Tiger: A Shaolin Fighting Art of North China*. New York: Weatherhill, 1997.

Yang Jwing-Ming. *Shaolin Long Fist Kung Fu*. Hollywood, CA: Unique Publications, 1981.

Index

About the Author

Christy Marx has written for television (*Babylon 5, Twilight Zone, Hypernauts*), animation (*X-Men: Evolution, Beast Wars, ReBoot, G.I. Joe, Spider-Man, Conan, Teenage Mutant Ninja Turtles, Jem*), computer games (*Legend of Alon D'ar*), and comic books (*Conan, Red Sonja, Sisterhood of Steel*). She has studied the martial arts of tae kwon do, shotokan, seven star praying mantis, and taijiquan. Visit her Web site at http://www.moonfire.to.

Photo Credits

Cover, pp. 58, 64–65, 68–69, 71, 73, 80–81, 83, 85 © The Everett Collection; pp. 4–5, 21, 22–23, 62, 75, 88 © AP/Wide World Photos; p. 8 © John T. Young/Corbis; pp. 16–17, 48–49 © Keren Su/Corbis; p. 32 © Bettmann/Corbis; pp. 38–39 © Wally McNamee/Corbis; p. 76 © Reuters New Media/Corbis.

Series Design and Layout

Les Kanturek